# HOTELES EN EL CAMPO

## COUNTRY HOTELS
## ALBERGHI DI CAMPAGNA
## HOTÉIS CAMPESTRES

**Editado por Macarena San Martín**

| | Art director: | Editorial coordination: |
|---|---|---|
| | Mireia Casanovas Soley | Simone Schleifer |
| Project coordination: | Texts: | Layout: |
| Macarena San Martín | Macarena San Martín | Francisco J. Castillo Moreno |

Translations coordination: Equipo de Edición, Barcelona
Translations:
Rachel Burden (English), Maria Elena Tondi, Olivia Papili (Italian), Escrítica Lda (Portuguese)

Editorial project:
2008 © LOFT Publications | Via Laietana, 32, 4.º, Of. 92 | 08003 Barcelona, Spain
Tel.: +34 932 688 088  Fax: +34 932 687 073 | loft@loftpublications.com | www.loftpublications.com

ISBN 978-84-96936-18-8     Printed in China

Cover photo: © Pere Planells
Back cover photo: © Manolo Yllera

LOFT affirms that it possesses all the necessary rights for the publication of this material and has duly paid all royalties related to the authors' and photographers' rights. LOFT also affirms that it has violated no property rights and has respected common law, all authors' rights and other rights that could be relevant. Finally, LOFT affirms that this book contains no obscene nor slanderous material.

The total or partial reproduction of this book without the authorization of the publishers violates the two rights reserved; any use must be requested in advance.

If you would like to propose works to include in our upcoming books, please email us at loft@loftpublications.com.

In some cases it has been impossible to locate copyright owners of the images published in this book. Please contact the publisher if you are the copyright owner of any of the images published here.

# HOTELES EN EL CAMPO

## COUNTRY HOTELS
## ALBERGHI DI CAMPAGNA
## HOTÉIS CAMPESTRES

**Editado por Macarena San Martín**

KOLON

"The real voyage of discovery consists not in seeking new landscapes but in having new eyes."

Marcel Proust, French novelist and author


"Il vero viaggio di scoperta non consiste nella ricerca di nuovi paesaggi, ma nell'avere occhi nuovi."

Marcel Proust, scrittore e romanziere francese

«El verdadero viaje del descubrimiento no consiste en buscar nuevos paisajes, sino en tener nuevos ojos».

Marcel Proust, escritor francés

"A verdadeira descoberta não reside na procura de novas paisagens, mas na contemplação do mundo com um olhar renovado".

Marcel Proust, escritor francês

12  SALOME'S GARDEN
    Tom Green, Nigel V. Brown

20  TIGMI
    Max Lawrence

30  DINAROBIN HOTEL
    Maurice Giraud

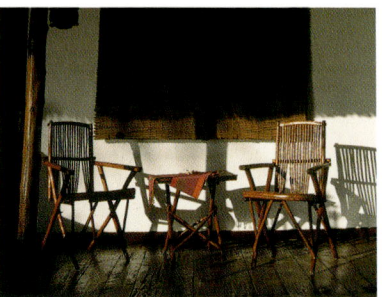

38  CHAPWANI PRIVATE ISLAND
    Maura Antonietto, Nigel V. Brown

44  RIAD ZINA MARRAKECH
    Max Lawrence

54  LAKE MANYARA TREE LODGE
    Chris Browne

62     DAR KAWA
       Quentin Vilboux

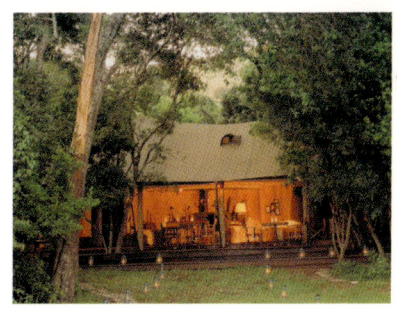

72     BATELEUR CAMP
       Chris Browne

78     GRUMETI RIVER CAMP
       Sylvio Rech

86     NOSSA SENHORA DA ASUNÇÃO POSADA
       José Paolo Santos

94     RIAD DAR AMANE
       Quentin Vilboux

102    CASAL DA DAMA
       Unknown

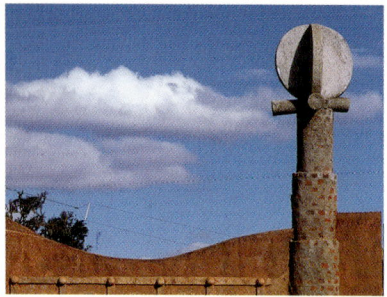

108    NGORONGORO CRATER LODGE
Silvio Rech & Lesley Carstens

120    QUINTA DO JUNCAL
Manuel Morgado
Ana Isabel Domingo

126    POSADA LA BONITA
Franco Martini

134    QUINTA DO CAMPO
Teresa Nunes da Ponte

142    LA SARACINA
Unknown

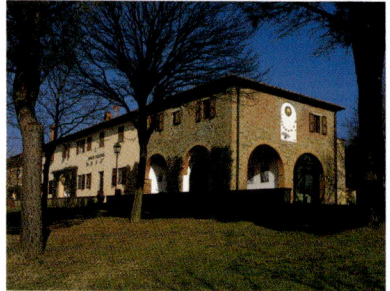

148    TENUTA SAN VITO
Unknown

158  HOSPEDERÍA CONVENTO LA PARRA
Francisco Viñao D'Lom
María Ulecia & Javier Muñoz

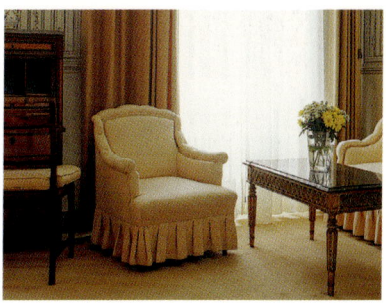

166  HOTEL TIVOLI PALACIO DE SETEAIS
Unknown

176  TORRE DI BELLOSGUARDO
Amerigo Franchetti

182  PIRÁ LODGE
Pablo Sánchez Elia
Laura Orcoyen

192  TENUTA LE VISTE
Rodolfo Bartoli

198  RESERVA ROTANA
Francisco Viñao D'Lom
María Ulecia & Javier Muñoz

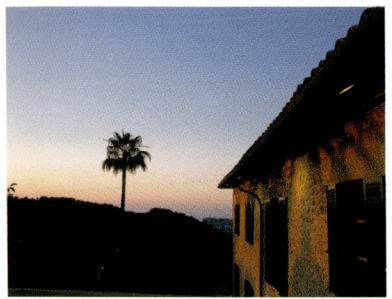

208    CA'S XORC
       Wolfgang Nikolaus Schmidt,
       Juan Puigserver, Mariano Barceló

216    CATACURIAN
       Unknown

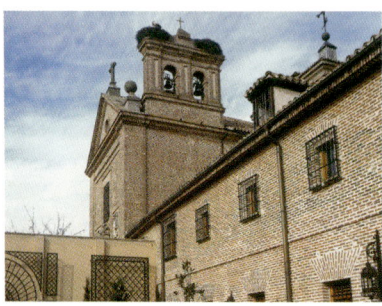

228    EL ANTIGUO CONVENTO DE BOADILLA
       DEL MONTE
       José Ramón Duralde

234    BAIA BENIAMIN
       M. Carlo Brunelli

240    LA LOCANDA DEL LOGGIATO
       Sabrina Marini

246    VILLA FONTELUNGA
       Philip Robinson

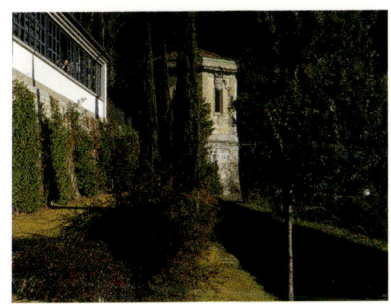

252 HOTEL VILLA FIESOLE
Bianchini

# SALOME'S GARDEN
The Last of the Royal Houses of Zanzibar

Architects: **Tom Green, Nigel V. Brown**

Date: 1997
Address: Bububu, 4 miles to the North of Stone Town, Zanzibar, Tanzania
More info tel.: +39 051 23 49 74  Fax: +39 01 23 90 86
www.salomes-garden.com
Photos: © Manolo Yllera

Style: rustic
Rooms: 4
Special features: large, unique rooms full of character. Private bathrooms, terrace, kitchen, central atrium and garden

# TIGMI
A Place of Quietude to Listen to Silence

## Architect: **Max Lawrence**

Address: Douar Tagadert el Kadi, Km 24 Route d'Amizmiz, Marrakech, Morocco
Tel.: +44 845 026 45 88
www.tigmi.com
Photos: © Pere Planells

Style: rustic
Rooms: 8
Special features: gardens, pool, terraces with 360° views, available on an exclusive basis for celebrating special occasions

# DINAROBIN HOTEL

## Golf & Spa, the Perfect Setting for Luxury Holidays in Mauritius

Architect: **Maurice Giraud**

Address: Le Morne Peninsula, Mauritius
Tel.: +11 230 401 49 00  Fax: +11 230 401 49 01
www.dinarobin-hotel.com
Photos: © Manolo Yllera

Style: tropical luxury
Rooms: 172 suites
Special features: golf course, land and sea sports, local band every night, miniclub, baby-sitter, boutiques, duty-free jewels, excursions, car hire, business center, conference facilities available

# CHAPWANI PRIVATE ISLAND
Discover the Real Magic of Zanzibar


Architects: **Maura Antonietto, Nigel V. Brown**

Address: Chapwani Island, Zanzibar, Tanzania
More info tel.: +39 051 23 49 74  Fax: +39 01 23 90 86
www.chapwaniisland.com
Photos: © Manolo Yllera

Style: rustic
Rooms: 10
Special features: Oriental, African and European cuisine restaurant, boat transfers, excursion organization, diving

# RIAD ZINA MARRAKECH
Your Hotel in Morocco

Architect: **Max Lawrence**

Address: Douar Tagadert el Kadi, Km 24 Route d'Amizmiz, Marrakech, Morocco
Tel.: +44 845 026 45 88
www.tigmi.com
Photos: © Pere Planells

Style: rustic
Rooms: 8
Special features: gardens, pool, terraces with 360° views, available on an exclusive basis for celebrating special occasions

# LAKE MANYARA TREE LODGE
## Luxury Safari Lodges on the Northern Tanzanian Safari Circuit

Architect: **Chris Browne**

Address: Lake Manyara National Park, Northern Tanzania
Tel.: +27 11 809 4300
www.lakemanyara.com
Photos: © CC Africa

Style: rustic luxury
Rooms: 10 treehouse suites
Special features: en suite bathroom and outdoor shower, private game viewing deck overlooking the forest, crafts gallery and swimming pool, tours and safaris

# DAR KAWA
## Bed and Breakfast in Morocco

Architect: **Quentin Vilboux**

Address: 18 Derb EjWalie Kaat Benahid, Marrakech, Morocco
Tel.: +212 24 42 80 79
Photos: © Manolo Yllera

Style: traditional
Rooms: 4
Special features: typical *riad* from the XVII century in the center of Marrakech

# BATELEUR CAMP
## Luxurious Tented Safari Accommodation

Architect: **Chris Browne**

Address: Kichwa Tembo, Masai Mara National Reserve, Kenya
Tel.: +27 11 809 43 14
www.ccafrica.com/accommodation-1-id-2-11/lodgeid-2-1
Photos: © CC Africa

Style: rustic luxury
Rooms: 32
Special features: expansive en suite bathrooms, fans, private butler service, elegant guest areas, lap pool, exciting safari activities

# GRUMETI RIVER CAMP
## Safari Accommodation at Grumeti

Architect: **Sylvio Rech**

Address: Western Serengeti, Tanzania
Tel.: +27 11 809 43 14
www.grumeti.com
Photos: © Manolo Yllera

Style: rustic
Rooms: tented suite
Special features: en suite bathrooms that offer separate WCs and alfresco showers which open to the sun and stars, safaris

# NOSSA SENHORA DA ASUNÇÃO POSADA

Perfect Harmony between Traditional and Modern Portugal

Architect: **José Paolo Santos**

Date: 1997
Address: Apartado 61, 7040 909 Arraiolos, Portugal
Tel.: +351 26 641 93 40  Fax: +351 26 641 92 80
www.portugalvirtual.pt/pousadas/arraiolos
Photos: © Pep Escoda

Style: traditional
Rooms: 2 intimate camps, each with 9 tented suites
Special features: restaurant, swimming pool, bar, air conditioning, tennis court, meeting room, horse riding

# RIAD DAR AMANE
Ideally Situated in the Center of Marrakech

Architect: **Quentin Vilboux**

Address: 33 Derb Mly Abdel Kader Derb Dabachi, 40000 Marrakech, Morocco
Photos: © Manolo Yllera

Style: rustic
Rooms: 4
Special features: safety deposit box, meeting/banquet facilities, baby-sitting, child services, solarium, internet services, fax/photocopying

# CASAL DA DAMA
Tourism in the Country


Architects: **Unknown**

Date: 1998
Address: Rua Tenente José Henrique 10, Toxofal de Cima, 2530 Lourinhã, Portugal
Tel.: +351 261 41 10 53  Fax: +351 261 42 32 00
www.maisturismo.pt
Photos: © Pep Escoda

Style: traditional
Rooms: 1 double and 3 singles
Special features: bar, snack bar, golf course (10 km), swimming pool, parking, tennis court

# NGORONGORO CRATER LODGE
## Sumptuous Safari Suites

Architects: **Silvio Rech & Lesley Carstens**

Address: Ngorongoro Crater, Serengeti National Park, Tanzania
Tel.: +27 11 809 43 14
www.ngorongorocrater.com
Photos: © CC Africa

Style: rustic luxury
Rooms: 3 intimate camps (2 with 12 suites, 1 with 6 suites)
Special features: fireplaces, exclusive butler service, safari shop, daily safaris to the Crater, birdwatching

# QUINTA DO JUNCAL
Manor Guest House

Architect: **Manuel Morgado**
Interior designer: **Ana Isabel Domingo**

Date: 1980, recently restored
Address: 2525 Serra D'el Rei, Peniche, Portugal
Tel.: +351 262 90 50 30  Fax: +351 262 90 53 01
www.quintadojuncal.com
Photos: © Pep Escoda

Style: traditional
Rooms: 8 rooms and 3 cabins
Special features: gift shop, swimming pool, tennis court, driving range, hiking, historical, cultural and gastronomic circuits

# POSADA LA BONITA
## An Unspoiled Eden in Deep, Luxurious Jungle

Interior designer: **Franco Martini**

Date: 1999
Address: Paraje el Soberbio, Misiones, Argentina
Tel.: +54 3755 68 03 80
www.posadalabonita.com.ar
Photos: © Virginia del Giudice

Style: rustic
Rooms: 3 jungle huts
Special features: horse riding, kayaking, canoeing, excursions to waterfalls

# QUINTA DO CAMPO
Tourism in a Manor House

Architect: **Teresa Nunes da Ponte (reconstruction)**

Date: 1994
Address: Rua Carles O'Neill 20, 2450-801 Valado dos Frades, Portugal
Tel.: +351 262 57 71 35  Fax: +351 262 57 75 55
www.quintadocampo.com
Photos: © Pep Escoda

Style: traditional
Rooms: 8 doubles and 7 suites
Special features: restaurant, self-service bar, cable TV, laundry, library, indoor games, gardens and pedestrian circuits, wedding and baptism celebrations

# LA SARACINA

The Country Home, Born from a Thought of Love and a Dream of Beauty

Architects: **Unknown**

Date: 1991
Address: S.S. 146 Km 29,7, 53026 Pienza, Siena, Italy
Tel.: +39 0578 74 80 22  Fax: +39 0578 74 80 18
www.lasaracina.it
Photos: © Pep Escoda

Style: traditional
Rooms: 3 suites, 2 doubles, 1 apartment
Special features: swimming pool, tennis court, jacuzzi, garden

# TENUTA SAN VITO

From the Land of Tuscany, the Warm Embrace of Beauty, Heart and Reason

Architects: **Unknown**

Date: 1985
Address: Via San Vito 59, 50056 Montelupo Florentino, Florence, Italy
Tel.: +39 0571 514 11  Fax: +39 0571 514 05
www.san-vito.com
Photos: © Pep Escoda

Style: traditional
Rooms: 4 apartments/villas
Special features: meeting lounge, swimming pool, weekly wine-tasting, mountain bikes

PODERE FRANTOIO

# HOSPEDERÍA CONVENTO LA PARRA

Creating a Pleasant Time for Our Guests

Architect: **Francisco Viñao D'Lom (restoration)**
Interior designers: **María Ulecia & Javier Muñoz**

Date: 2000
Address: Santa María 16, La Parra, 06176 Badajoz, Spain
Tel.: +34 924 68 26 92  Fax: +34 924 68 26 19
www.laparra.net
Photos: © Pep Escoda

Style: traditional
Rooms: 21
Special features: gift shop, outdoor activities, cooking classes, convention room, swimming pool

# HOTEL TIVOLI PALACIO DE SETEAIS

Stunning Scenery and a Spectacular Setting

Architects: **Unknown**

Date: 1996
Address: Rua Barbosa du Bocage 10, Sintra 2710-517, Lisbon, Portugal
Tel.: +351 21 923 32 00  Fax: +351 21 923 42 77
www.tivolihotels.com
Photos: © Pep Escoda

Style: luxurious
Rooms: 30
Special features: restaurant, bar, laundry service, safe, baby-sitting, swimming pool, parking

# TORRE DI BELLOSGUARDO

Hospitality and a Unique Atmosphere

Owner: **Amerigo Franchetti**
Interior designer: **Amerigo Franchetti**

Date: 1996
Address: Via Roti Michelozzi 2, 50124 Florence, Italy
Tel.: +39 055 229 81 45  Fax: +39 055 22 90 08
www.torrebellosguardo.com
Photos: © Pep Escoda

Style: traditional
Rooms: 8 doubles, 7 suites, 1 single
Special features: cooking classes, sports center, sauna, massage, flower garden, vegetable garden, vineyard, olive groves

# PIRÁ LODGE
In Search of Gold

Architect: **Pablo Sánchez Elia**
Interior designer: **Laura Orcoyen**

Date: 2000
Address: Pasaje de El Boquerón, Mercedes, Corrientes, Argentina
Tel.: +54 1143 31 97 10  Fax: +54 3773 42 03 99
www.piralodge.com
Photos: © Virginia del Giudice

Style: rustic
Rooms: 5 doubles
Special features: kayaking, fly fishing, horse riding

# TENUTA LE VISTE
Florence: Charming Luxury Hotel

Interior designer: **Rodolfo Bartoli**

Date: 1996
Address: Via del Leone 11, 50028 Mosciano, Florence, Italy
Tel.: +39 055 76 85 43  Fax: +39 055 76 82 19
www.tenuta-leviste.it
Photos: © Pep Escoda

Style: luxurious
Rooms: 4 doubles
Special features: satellite TV, huge park with olive trees and swimming pool, own oil production

# RESERVA ROTANA

Feel at Home in a Charming 17th Century Mansion

Architect: **Francisco Viñao D'Lom (restoration)**
Interior designers: **María Ulecia & Javier Muñoz**

Date: 1996
Address: Camí de S'Avall, Km 3, 07500 Manacor, Majorca, Spain
Tel.: +34 971 84 56 85  Fax: +34 971 55 52 58
www.reservarotana.com
Photos: © Pep Escoda

Style: traditional
Rooms: 22
Special features: minibar, satellite TV, air conditioning, heating, wine cellar, golf course

# CA'S XORC

Enjoy Complete Well-being in an Incomparable Environment

Architects: **Wolfgang Nikolaus Schmidt, Juan Puigserver, Mariano Barceló**

Date: 2000
Address: Carretera de Deià, Km 56,1, 07100 Soller, Majorca, Spain
Tel.: +34 971 63 82 80  Fax: +34 971 63 29 49
www.casxorc.com
Photos: © Pep Escoda

Style: rustic
Rooms: 10 doubles
Special features: swimming pools, gardens, convention room with audiovisual equipment, jacuzzi, sauna and steam bath

# CATACURIAN
## Gourmet Food & Wine Boutique Hotel

Architects: **Unknown**

Address: Progrès 2, 43736 El Masroig, Tarragona, Spain
Tel.: +34 977 82 53 41  Fax: +34 977 27 05 61
www.catacurian.net
Photos: © Pep Escoda

Style: traditional
Rooms: 18
Special features: restaurant and bar, cooking classes, visits to local wineries

# EL ANTIGUO CONVENTO DE BOADILLA DEL MONTE

Cozy Atmosphere Surrounded by Magnificent Countryside

Architect: **José Ramón Duralde**

Address: Calle de las Monjas s/n, 28660 Boadilla del Monte, Madrid, Spain
Tel.: +34 916 32 22 20  Fax: +34 916 33 15 12
www.elconvento.net
Photos: © Pep Escoda

Style: traditional
Rooms: 18
Special features: restaurant, music and DJ services, wine tasting courses

# BAIA BENIAMIN
## Everything to Satisfy the Customers' Wishes

Interior designer: **M. Carlo Brunelli**

Date: 1986
Address: Corso Europa 63, Grimaldi Inferiore, Ventimiglia, Italy
Tel.: +39 0184 380 02  Fax: +39 0184 380 27
www.baiabeniamin.it
Photos: © Pep Escoda

Style: traditional luxury
Rooms: 5 doubles
Special features: safe, minibar, restaurant, bar, breakfast on the terrace overlooking the bay, wine cellar, private beach, garden

36

IL LOGGIATO

# LA LOCANDA DEL LOGGIATO

Medieval Village in Val d'Orcia

Owner: **Sabrina Marini**
Architect: **Sabrina Marini**
Interior designer: **Sabrina Marini**

Date: 2000
Address: Piazza del Moretto 30, Bagno Vignoni, Siena, Italy
Tel.: +39 0577 88 89 25
www.loggiato.it
Photos: © Pep Escoda

Style: rustic
Rooms: 6 doubles
Special features: each room has its own atmosphere, wine bar, wine cellar, thermal water pools

# VILLA FONTELUNGA
Home Away from Home

Interior designer: **Philip Robinson**

Date: 2000
Address: Via Cunicchio 5, 52045 Arezzo, Tuscany, Italy
Tel.: +39 0575 66 04 10  Fax: +39 0575 66 19 63
www.fontelunga.com
Photos: © Pep Escoda

Style: rustic luxury
Rooms: 8 doubles, 1 twin
Special features: continental breakfast, air conditioning, laundry, modern en suite showers and bathrooms, swimming pool

# HOTEL VILLA FIESOLE
A Luxury Hotel in Tuscany

Architect: **Bianchini**
Interior designer: **Bianchini**

Date: 1995
Address: Via Beato Angelico 35, 50014 Florence, Italy
Tel.: +39 055 59 72 52  Fax: +39 055 59 91 33
www.villafiesole.it
Photos: © Pep Escoda

Style: luxurious
Rooms: 28 doubles
Special features: restaurant, bar, internet, laundry, massages, wedding celebrations